HUNTER AND ME
– Best Buds

"A STORY BOOK FOR CHILDREN"

Written by:
Mr. Bryce Allan Holland

Bryce

was a Marine Corps
veteran but he felt very sad

Hunter

was a silver German Shepherd, the
shelter said he was bad

Bryce looked

in his cage and saw Hunter was cold

The shelter said, you don't want this
dog because he's very old
But Bryce looked in his eyes and saw
a heart of gold

He said give him a blanket
and I'll take him home

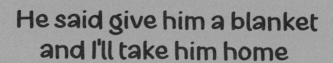
He will have a big back yard where
he can roam

The shelter was no place for

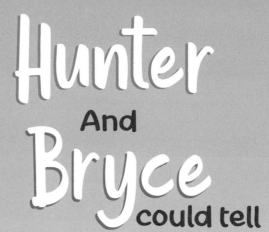

Hunter
And
Bryce
could tell

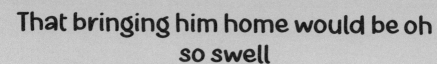
That bringing him home would be oh
so swell

Hunter

was skinny and Bryce didn't like
how he was treated

So, they went to the store and
got everything he needed

He bought a dog bed, some
good food and some toys

Hunter
felt like he was one of the boys

But it was much more than
that, they were

Best Friends

Hunter knew they would be
friends until the end

When they got home Bryce said
"no dogs on the bed"

But he woke up laying right
next to that sleepy head

It warmed Bryce's
heart and from
there it was a wrap

He let Hunter sleep
on his bed even for naps

Although Hunter was old
his energy was high

He took Bryce to play all day
and all night

It didn't matter if it
was summer, winter,
spring or fall

You could always
find Hunter & Bryce
throwing the ball

They were always so
happy when they were
together

They played outside all
the time, no matter the
weather

Bryce
took hunter to mountains,
the rivers, and lakes

He even took hunter to buy
Birthday Cakes

Hunter loved Bryce
& had to look no further

Every year
for his birthday he got a
bacon cheeseburger

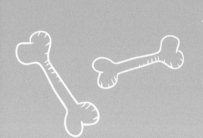

They went to the mountains to look at the stars

He always sat next to Bryce in the car

Hunter

was the best dog Bryce could have asked for

It made them so happy, and they both loved to explore

When they woke up in the
mornings they always
would play

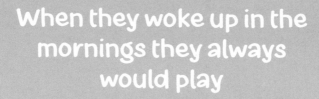

And they both knew it
would be a

Great Day

Everywhere Bryce went,
Hunter followed him
around

Hunter

always reminded Bryce
never to frown

As they both got older and couldn't play as much

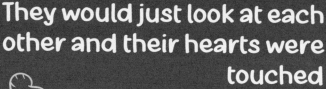

They would just look at each other and their hearts were touched

They both felt blessed to have one another

they were never alone because they were like brothers

They would go on hikes
in the mountains and
watch the sun go down

Sunsets

like these were best in
town

He was such a good dog
and was always re-
minded

If there was a better
place on earth, no one
could find it

Alongside Bryce was the
best place to be

They went on so many
Adventures,
it felt good to be free

Everyone says they have the
best dog, and everyone is
right

But the best dog in the
world belongs to
Bryce

Hunter

knows this, because he got treats every morning

And life with Bryce was never boring

Bryce

used to think things were falling apart

But because of Hunter, Love filled his heart

Hunter

thought of the shelter,
and he'd never go back

Bryce

set him free, and he
loved his new path

That Marine saved me, I'm
so free and its nice

But who really saved who?
I think
Hunter saved Bryce